SR MARIE-PA

Mother of Mercy

A Month with Mary

ST PAULS

MARY,
THE NEW EVE

From the Book of Genesis (3:14-15)

The LORD God said to the serpent,
"Because you have done this,
cursed are you among all animals
and among all wild creatures; (...)
I will put enmity between you and the woman,
and between your offspring and hers;
he will strike your head,
and you will strike his heel."

Comment

The knot of Eve's disobedience was untied by the
obedience of Mary; what the virgin Eve bound by her
disbelief, the Virgin Mary loosened with her faith.

Irenaeus of Lyons, II century

PRAYER

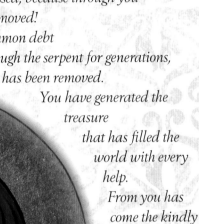

Blessed are you, O Mary,
you became the mother of the Lord of kings!
In your womb dwelt the One for whom
the heavens are filled with praise.
Blessed are you, O Blessed, because through you
the curse of Eve was removed!
Thanks to you, the common debt
      contracted through the serpent for generations,
           has been removed.
             You have generated the
               treasure
                 that has filled the
                  world with every
                    help.
                     From you has
                     come the kindly
                     light
                     that destroyed
                     the kingdom of
                     darkness.

                  Ephraim the Syrian,
                      VI century

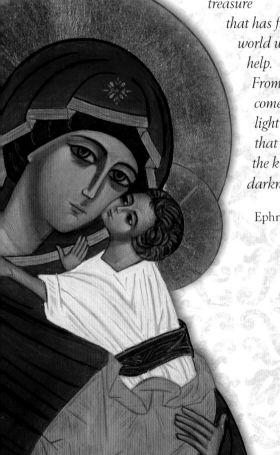

MARY, FLAME OF GOD

From the Book of Exodus (3:4-6)

God called to (Moses) out of the bush, "Moses, Moses!" And he said, "Here I am." Then he said, "Come no closer! Remove the sandals from your feet, for the place on which you are standing is holy ground." He said further, "I am the God of your father, the God of Abraham, the God of Isaac, and the God of Jacob." And Moses hid his face, for he was afraid to look at God.

Comment

What was foreshadowed in the flame and in the bush was openly manifested in the mystery of the Virgin. As on the mountain the bush burned but was not consumed, so the Virgin gave birth to the light but remained a virgin. The similarity with the bush is not unseemly: it prefigures the body of the Virgin, who gave birth to God.

Gregory of Nyssa, IV century

PRAYER

Mary, you are the bush
seen by Moses
that was not consumed
by the flames,
which were the Son of God.
He came and lived in your womb
and the fire of his divinity
did not consume your flesh.
Pray for us, O Saint!

Hymn of the
Ethiopian Church

MARY, THE STRONG WOMAN

From the Book of Judges (5:7-8, 12)

There were valiant leaders in Israel, they ceased,
Until you, Deborah, arose,
Until you arose as a mother in Israel.
New gods were chosen;
Then war was in the gates.
Not a shield or a spear was seen
Among forty thousand in Israel. (...)
Awake, awake, Deborah;
Awake, awake, sing a song!
Arise, Barak, and take away your captives,
O son of Abinoam.

Comment

The true path to follow to find a bridge between
Deborah and Mary of Nazareth is a fundamental
theological motif that we must repeat for many other
women in the Old Testament (Ruth, Anna, Esther,
Judith). This motif is expressed well by St Paul: God
chose what is low and despised in the world, things that
are not, to reduce to nothing things that are
(1 Cor 1:27-28).

Gianfranco Ravasi

PRAYER

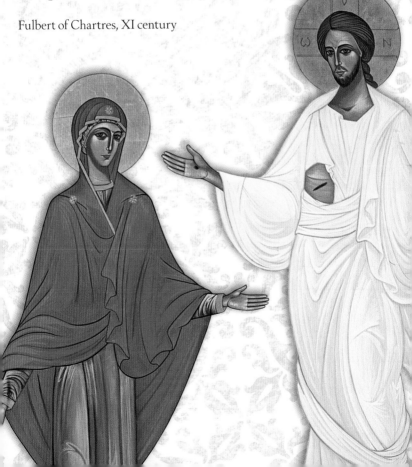

Holy Mary, comforter of the afflicted,
encourager of the disheartened, strength of the weak.
Those who celebrate your memory
experience all of your generous help.
Be attentive to the voice of those who pray.
Satisfy the desires of all.
It is your role to intercede constantly for the people of God,
you who merited, or were blessed,
to carry out the redemption of the world,
through him who lives and reigns forever and ever!

Fulbert of Chartres, XI century

MARY,
FULL OF GRACE

From the Book of Judges (6:14-15, 36-38)

Then the LORD turned to (Gideon) and said, "Go in this might of yours and deliver Israel from the hand of Midian; I hereby commission you." He responded, "But sir, how can I deliver Israel? My clan is the weakest in Manasseh, and I am the least in my family." (...) Then Gideon said to God, "If now I have found favor in your eyes, then show me a sign that it is you who speak with me (...) I am going to lay a fleece of wool on the threshing-floor; if there is dew on the fleece alone, and it is dry on all the ground, then I shall know that you will deliver Israel by my hand, as you have said." And it was so. When he rose early next morning and squeezed the fleece, he wrung enough dew from the fleece to fill a bowl with water.

Comment

With what words of praise will I illustrate the immaculate character of the purity of Mary? She is the immaculate fleece placed in the farmyard of the world, from which the Savior, descending from the sky like rain, dried up the earth from the immense flowering of evils and again drained the fleece underlying the humidity of the passions and filled the land with the overflowing gift of goodness.

Pseudo-Proclus of Constantinople,
IX century

PRAYER

O Christ, God, the Word of the Father, you have come down like rain on the field of the Virgin and, as a grain of perfect wheat, you have appeared where no one had ever sown and you became food for the world ... We praise you, Virgin Mother of God, fleece that absorbed the dew of heaven, field of blessed wheat that satisfies the hunger of creation.

Hymn of praise of the
Syro-Maronite Church

MARY,
FAITHFUL WOMAN

From the Book of Ruth (4:13, 17)

So Boaz took Ruth and she became his wife. When they came together, the LORD made her conceive, and she bore a son. (...) They named him Obed; he became the father of Jesse, the father of David.

Comment

From pagan stock arose that virtuous woman who was Ruth the Moabite, who abandoned the gods, their errors, and her people, and who received an inheritance in the land of Israel by right of kinship. From Boaz' descendants the savior Jesus was conceived of the Virgin Mary. In his mercy the Lord, who took account from afar, praised him, saying, "Judah is my scepter; Moab is my wash-basin."

Osbert of Clare, XII century

PRAYER

In the presence of all the heavenly court this day I choose you, O Mary, for my Mother and Queen. I offer and consecrate to you, in full submission and love, my body and soul, my goods, both interior and exterior, and even the value of all my good actions, past, present and future; leaving entirely to you the full right of the disposing of me, and all that belongs to me, without exception, according to your will, for the greater glory of God in time and in eternity.

St. Louis de Montfort (1673-1716)

MARY,
HUMBLE SERVANT OF THE LORD

From the First Book of Samuel (1:20; 2:1)

In due time Hannah conceived and bore a son. She named him Samuel, for she said, "I have asked him of the LORD." (...) Hannah prayed and said, "My heart exults in the LORD; my strength is exalted in my God. My mouth derides my enemies, because I rejoice in your victory."

Comment

He who gives the seed to the man, inhabits the body of the Virgin; he who made the sterile Sarah fruitful, dwells in the womb of the daughter of David. The One who has kept watch over the tears of Hannah, has also seen the humility of Mary. The One who has removed a rib from Adam, has lowered himself to enter this same rib of Adam.

Isaac of Antioch, V century

PRAYER

Hail, full of grace:
the curse is over,
corruption is dissolved,
sadness has ceased,
joy has flourished,
in you the good news of the prophets has been realized.

Gregory of Nyssa,
IV Century

MARY,
ARK OF THE NEW COVENANT

From the Second Book of Samuel (6:2, 9-11)

David and all the people with him set out and went (...) to bring up from there the ark of God, which is called by the name of the LORD of hosts who is enthroned on the cherubim. (...) David was afraid of the LORD that day; he said, "How can the ark of the LORD come into my care?" So David (...) took it to the house of Obed-edom the Gittite. The ark of the LORD remained in the house of Obed-edom the Gittite for three months; and the LORD blessed Obed-edom and all his household.

Comment

The ark of Israel was made of wood but was plated with gold inside and out. For the people of Israel the gold and wood symbolized the union of divinity with humanity. Gold-plated inside and out, the ark is also a symbol of Mary, the Holy Mother of God: on the outside it symbolizes the irreproachability of Mary, far from any impurities and shamelessness, on the inside it symbolizes the Holy Spirit, who must live in all intimacy.

John of Dara, IX century

PRAYER

All praise you as the temple of the Living,
O mother of God!
Rejoice, tent of God and his Word,
saint most exalted of saints,
golden ark of the Spirit,
inexhaustible treasure of life!
Rejoice, precious diadem of saintly kings,
unshakeable tower of the Church!

Acclamation of the Byzantine liturgy

MARY,
VIRGIN DAUGHTER OF SION

From the Book of the prophet Zephaniah (3:14-15, 17)

Sing aloud, O daughter Zion;
shout, O Israel!
Rejoice and exult with all your heart,
O daughter Jerusalem!
The LORD has taken away the judgments against you;
he has turned away your enemies.
The king of Israel, the LORD, is in your midst;
You shall fear disaster no more ...
he will rejoice over you with gladness,
he will renew you in his love;
he will exult over you with loud singing
as on a day of festival.

Comment

The daughter of Zion who, according to the prophetic announcements, personified the community of the covenant, is the direct collaborator of the Lord in fulfilling the Messianic salvation, welcoming the Savior and giving life to the new people of God. After suffering and abandonment in which it seemed that the hopes of Israel were buried, everything flourished in a prodigious way.

Alberto Valentini

PRAYER

Hail, O habitation of the divinity,
the one whom the heavens cannot contain
is contained in your womb, O Blessed!
Hail, fiery throne!
Hail, daughter of Zion, intact mountain:
   you live in the fullness of the Godhead
   by the will of the Eternal Father
   and through the intervention of the
   Holy Spirit!
      Hail, full of grace, the
      Lord is with you!

Anatolius,
VII century

MARY, VICTORIOUS OVER EVIL

From the Book of Judith (15:9-10)

"You are the glory of Jerusalem, you are the surpassing joy of Israel, you are the splendid boast of our people! You have done all this with your own hand; you have done good to Israel, and God is pleased with what you have wrought. May the Almighty Lord bless you forever!" And all the people answered, "Amen!"

Comment

At that time the Savior turned to Mary, and said, "For you, my Mother, I will do what I have not done for anyone, because you have generated me for the salvation of the world. When the water of your tears flow, when I see your dove-like eyes shedding hot tears, I am deeply moved within. The fire of my wrath is cooled, my anger is pacified, my mercy is bestowed unexpectedly, and my clemency extends wherever you will."

Pact of Mercy, XVIII century

PRAYER

Under your protection we take refuge,
O Holy Mother of God;
despise not the petitions
of us who are put to the test
but deliver us from every danger,
O glorious and blessed Virgin.

Prayer composed in Egypt, III century
(in Latin Sub tuum praesidium)

MARY,
OUR ADVOCATE

From the Book of Esther (7:3-4)

Then Queen Esther answered, "If I have won your favor, O king, and if it pleases the king, let my life be given me—that is my petition—and the lives of my people. For we have been sold, I and my people, to be destroyed, to be killed, to be annihilated."

Comment

"I will make you as a wall of the world, a bulwark for those shaken by large waves, an ark of those who are saved, a staff for those who let themselves be led by the hand, intercession for sinners and stairs that have the power to take people up to heaven."

Germanus of Constantinople, VIII century

O Queen, help us,
move yourself to pity,
be quick,
we are going to succumb
under the weight of sin.
Do not remain disappointed with your servants
For you alone are our hope!
If you were not able to intercede for us,
who would free us from so many dangers?
Who would have preserved us
immune up to now?
O Queen, we are never forsaken
by you;
you always save your servants
from every misfortune.

Hymn of the
Greek Church

MARY,
SPLENDOR OF GRACE

From the Book of Psalms (45:1, 9-11)

My heart overflows with a goodly theme;
I address my verses to the king; (...)
daughters of kings are among your ladies of honor;
at your right hand stands the queen in gold of Ophir.

Hear, O daughter, consider and incline your ear;
forget your people and your father's house,
and the king will desire your beauty.
Since he is your lord, pay homage to him.

Comment

Listen, O daughter, and turn your ear to the message of
Gabriel, because it is exactly due to this message that
we have cancelled, as one cancels a bitter sound with a
sweet discourse, the poison of disobedience (that the
astute serpent had instilled in the ears of Eve and made
all of humanity share in the poisonous drop) and have
been made capable of submitting ourselves and obeying
only the commandments of our Creator.

Photius of Constantinople, IX century

PRAYER

Your ways, O Blessed Virgin
Mother of God, amaze the heavens;
You have borne and carried on your bosom
the One who with a single nod
governs all creatures.
O Bride of the King,
ask and petition the One
you have borne
with all purity,
to spread his mercy,
on the day of your feast,
upon all those who take
refuge
in your prayers.

Invocation of the Church

MARY, SEAT OF WISDOM

From the Book of Wisdom (9:1-2, 4-6)

"O God of my ancestors and Lord of mercy,
who have made all things by your word,
and by your wisdom have formed humankind (...)
give me the wisdom that sits by your throne,
and do not reject me from among your servants.
For I am your servant, the son of your handmaid,
a man who is weak and short-lived,
with little understanding of judgment and of laws;
for even if one be perfect among human beings
he will be regarded as nothing if he is without the
wisdom that comes from you."

Comment

The Virgin loved to learn and was a good disciple,
conserving in her heart every good word. Her heart
was full of reflection on the divine Scriptures, full of all
wisdom: she had in fact become the Mother of the Word
and of the Wisdom of God, open to the word and able to
communicate by voice the message transmitted to her.

Maximus the Confessor, VII century

PRAYER

O Mary, my Lady,
you are the garden of wisdom,
whose flower neither falls nor dies.
O beautiful spouse,
that shines more than the beauty of the sun,
ignite in my heart
the lamp of wisdom and prudence.
Be watchful in keeping me and ready to defend me!

Ethiopian hymn,
XVI century

MARY, INTACT GARDEN

From the Song of Songs (4:7, 9-10, 12)

You are altogether beautiful, my love;
there is no flaw in you. (...)
You have ravished my heart, my sister, my bride,
you have ravished my heart with a glance of your eyes,
with one jewel of your necklace.
How sweet is your love, my sister, my bride!
how much better is your love than wine,
and the fragrance of your oils than any spice. (...)
A garden locked is my sister, my bride,
a garden locked, a fountain sealed.

Comment

Mary is the only one who merited to be called both "mother" and "spouse" [of the one person]. While the mother of our kind brought pain into the world, the Mother of our Lord has brought salvation. Eve, by disobedience, brought harm; Mary, by giving life, has brought benefit. Eve has struck, Mary has healed. The Virgin, in fact, admirably and ineffably generated the Savior, of herself and of all things. She is the temple of God, the designated font, the gateway in the house of the Lord!

Ambrose Autpert, VIII century

PRAYER

O God, you have made the womb
of the Virgin Mary a sealed fountain.
You yourself enter and leave
the closed garden of the Mother
in a way that does not violate the virginity of the Generatrix,
please prepare us to be the garden of your good will,
that you alone can inhabit
where you gather the fruits of virtue.

Visigothic Prayer

MARY,
VIRGIN OF VIRGINS

From the Book of the Prophet Isaiah (7:13-15; 9:2)

Then Isaiah said, "Hear then, O house of David! Is it not enough for you to weary men, must you weary my God as well? Therefore the Lord himself will give you a sign. Behold, the virgin is with child and shall bear a son, and shall name him Immanuel. He shall eat curds and honey by the time he knows how to refuse the evil and choose the good." (...)
"The people who walked in darkness
have seen a great light;
those who lived in a land of deep darkness –
on them light has shone."

Comment

"The virgin shall conceive", sang Isaiah. But he did not explain to whom, or where and when it would happen. In Mary the voice of prophecy sounded loud, because it was made known in her, full of prodigious portents... The mysteries concealed in the prophetic books were made clear in Mary. From her arose the sun of justice and at her rising she illumined all the earth... In Mary all the symbols and signs have been fulfilled; the prophetic announcements have been realized in her.

Ephraim the Syrian, IV century

PRAYER

O Immaculate Virgin,
mother of God and full of grace,
the One you have carried is Immanuel,
the fruit of your womb.
You, O Mary, are above all praise!
I greet you, Mary,
mother of God and glory
of the angels,
because you surpass
in fullness of grace
all the pronouncements
of the prophets!
The Lord is with you:
you bring forth
the Savior of the world.

Ancient invocation,
III century

MARY,
VIRGIN EARTH

From the Book of the Prophet Isaiah (61:10; 62:4-5)

I will greatly rejoice in the LORD,
my whole being shall exult in my God; (...)
You shall no more be named Forsaken,
and your land shall no more be named Desolate;
but you shall be called My Delight Is In Her,
and your land Married;
for the LORD delights in you,
and your land shall be married.
For as a young man marries a young woman,
so shall your God marry you,
and as the bridegroom rejoices over his bride,
so shall your God rejoice over you.

Comment

From where comes the substance of the first man?
From the will and wisdom of God and from the virgin
earth. From this earth God took clay and formed man,
the beginning of the human race. By being born of a
virgin, the Lord, through the will and wisdom of God,
reproduced the same schema of corporeality to show the
sameness of his corporeality with that of Adam and to
remake, as in the beginning, man in the image of God.

Irenaeus of Lyons, II century

PRAYER

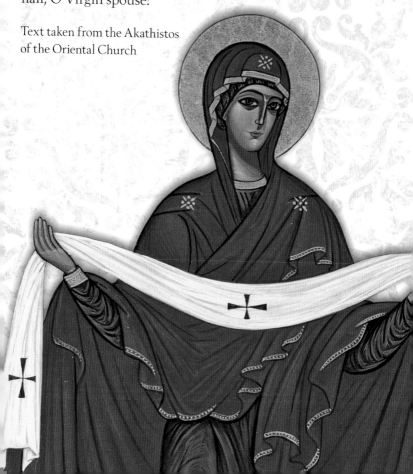

Hail, O shoot of a trunk not dried up,
hail, O mother of the creator of our life,
hail, O fruitful earth that brings forth mercy,
hail, O table prepared with abundant gifts,
hail, O you who make the garden of delights to flower,
hail, O you who prepares for souls a sure haven,
hail, O pardon for the entire world,
hail, O divine benevolence for mortals,
hail, O confident word of mortals addressed to God,
hail, O Virgin spouse!

Text taken from the Akathistos
of the Oriental Church

MARY, FULL OF GRACE

From the Gospel according to Luke (1:26-31)

In the sixth month [of Elizabeth's pregnancy], the angel Gabriel was sent by God to a town in Galilee called Nazareth, to a virgin engaged to a man whose name was Joseph, of the house of David. The virgin's name was Mary. And he came to her and said, "Greetings, full of grace! The Lord is with you." But she was greatly troubled by his words and pondered what sort of greeting this might be. The angel said to her, "Do not be afraid, Mary, for you have found favor with God. And now, you will conceive in your womb and bear a son, and you will name him Jesus."

Comment

The angel waits for your response, O Mary! In your hands is the price of our rescue. Answer quickly, O Virgin! Say, O Lady, the word that the earth and the lower regions and even heaven are expecting. Give your word and receive the Word... Open, therefore, O blessed Virgin, your heart to faith, your lips to the word, your womb to the Creator. Behold, the one desired by all the nations stands outside and knocks at your door... Arise, run and open! Arise with your faith, run with your affection, open with your consent!

St. Bernard of Clairvaux (1090-1153)

PRAYER

Hail, O full of grace, the Lord is with you!
Hail, dwelling of the divinity,
he whom the heavens cannot contain,
is contained in your womb, O Blessed One!
In you, in fact, dwells the fullness of divinity
by the will of the eternal Father
and through the intervention of the Holy Spirit!
Hail, O full of grace, the Lord is with you!

Anatolius, VII century

MARY,
BLESSED AMONG WOMEN

From the Gospel according to Luke (1:41-44)

When Elizabeth heard Mary's greeting, the child leapt in her womb. And Elizabeth was filled with the Holy Spirit and exclaimed with a loud cry, "Blessed are you among women, and blessed is the fruit of your womb! And why has this happened to me that the mother of my Lord comes to me? For as soon as I heard the sound of your greeting, the child in my womb leapt for joy!"

Comment

Mary greeted Elizabeth: the mother of the master greeted the mother of the servant; the mother of the king greeted the mother of the soldier; the mother of God greeted the mother of the man; the virgin greeted the married woman. And when they greeted each other, the Holy Spirit that dwelt in the womb of Mary prompted the one in the womb of Elizabeth, as one prompts his own friend, "Hasten to arise! Come out, make straight the ways of Christ, that he may accomplish the salvation entrusted to him!"

St. Athanasius, IV century

PRAYER

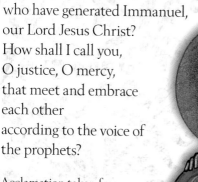

How shall I call you, O virgin all holy?
How shall I call you, O city of the great King,
ornate castle of the King of kings?
How shall I call you, lofty and holy stairway,
at whose top is found the Lord
whom the angels glorify?
How shall I call you, O blessed among women,
who have generated Immanuel,
our Lord Jesus Christ?
How shall I call you,
O justice, O mercy,
that meet and embrace
each other
according to the voice of
the prophets?

Acclamation taken from
the Coptic liturgy

MARY,
CAUSE OF OUR JOY

From the Gospel according to Luke (1:46-50)

And Mary said,
"My soul magnifies the Lord,
and my spirit rejoices in God my Savior,
for he has looked with favor on his lowly servant.
Surely, from now on all generations will call me blessed;
for the Mighty One has done great things for me,
and holy is his name.
His mercy is for those who fear him
from generation to generation."

Comment

In the Magnificat, Mary teaches us how we must love and praise God, with a liberated spirit, without seeking in him our interest... Mary wants you to reach God through her, learning to hope and confide in him. She wants to be the greatest example of the grace of God so as to incite everybody to confidence and to the praise of divine grace.

Martin Luther (1483-1546)

PRAYER

O blessed Virgin, mother of God,
What a great consolation
God has shown us in you!
Since with so much grace
he has looked upon your humility and nothingness,
reminding us that from now on
he will not despise,
but look graciously on we poor men and women,
according to your example.

Martin Luther

MARY,
SPOUSE OF JOSEPH

From the Gospel according to Matthew (1:20-21)

An angel of the Lord appeared to him in a dream and said, "Joseph, son of David, do not be afraid to take Mary as your wife, for the child conceived in her is from the Holy Spirit. She will bear a son, and you are to name him Jesus, for he will save his people from their sins."

Comment

With these words the angel obliterated the doubt suffered by Joseph and at the same time stirred a new fear in him, that of esteeming and reverencing even more the holy Virgin as one full of the Holy Spirit and mother according to the flesh of the sublime and ineffable Son, born before the ages, who would save his people from their sins.

Maximus the Confessor, VII century

PRAYER

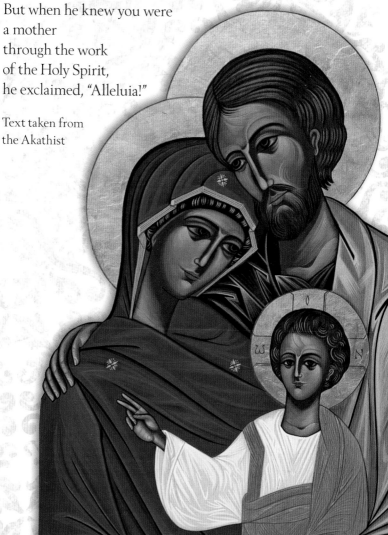

Experiencing in himself a tempest
of contrasting thoughts,
the righteous Joseph was disturbed.
Knowing he did not touch you,
he suspected you,
the irreproachable one, of furtive loves!
But when he knew you were
a mother
through the work
of the Holy Spirit,
he exclaimed, "Alleluia!"

Text taken from
the Akathist

MARY, WOMB OF THE WORD MADE FLESH

From the Gospel according to Luke (2:4-7)

Joseph went from the town of Nazareth in Galilee to Judea, to the city of David called Bethlehem, because he was descended from the house and family of David. He went to be registered with Mary, to whom he was engaged and who was expecting a child. While they were there, the time came for her to deliver her child. And she gave birth to her firstborn son and wrapped him in bands of cloth, and laid him in a manger, because there was no room for them in the inn.

Comment

The author of life was born of our flesh from the Mother of the living. With his swaddling clothes he unties the chains of our sins and wipes away for good the tears of our mothers. Dance and exult, creation of the Lord, for your Savior is born... I contemplate a strange and unexpected mystery: the grotto is heaven, the Virgin is the throne of the cherubim, the manger is the place where the incomprehensible one rests: the Christ God.

Antiphon of the Byzantine Liturgy

PRAYER

How much light for the world,
what grace for all heaven!
What splendor when Christ
came out from the womb of Mary,
a splendor never seen!
Hail, holy Mother,
you have given birth
to the king,
the one who rules
heaven
and earth in time,
and whose dominion
is without end.

Coelius Sedulius,
V century

MARY,
CONSOLER OF THE AFFLICTED

From the Gospel according to Luke (2:22, 33-35)

When the time came for their purification according to the Law of Moses, they brought him up to Jerusalem to present him to the Lord. (...) And the child's father and mother were amazed at what was said about him. Then Simeon blessed them and said to his mother Mary, "This child is destined for the fall and the rise of many in Israel, and to be a sign that will be opposed, so that the inner thoughts of many will be revealed—and a sword will pierce your own soul too."

Comment

When Christ cried out, "My God, my God, why have you abandoned me?" the virgin Mary must also have been pierced by a suffering that humanly corresponded to that of her Son. "A sword shall pierce your own soul and the thoughts of many hearts will be revealed"; also your soul, if you still dare to believe, if you are still humble enough to believe that in truth you are the chosen one among women, the one who has found grace before God.

Søren Kierkegaard (1813-1855)

PRAYER

At the Cross her station keeping,
stood the mournful Mother weeping,
close to her Son to the last.
Through her heart, His sorrow sharing,
all His bitter anguish bearing,
now at length the sword has passed...
O thou Mother! Fount of love!
Touch my spirit from above,
make my heart with thine accord.
Make me feel as thou hast felt;
make my soul to glow
and melt
with the love
of Christ my
Lord

From the
Stabat Mater
of Jacopone
da Todi,
XIII century

MARY,
STAR OF HEAVEN

From the Gospel according to Matthew (2:1-2)

In the time of King Herod, after Jesus was born in Bethlehem of Judea, wise men from the East came to Jerusalem asking, "Where is the child who has been born king of the Jews? For we observed his star at its rising, and have come to pay him homage."

Comment

The light that has risen from darkness is Christ... but among those people resembling the night, the Virgin Mary was not night; rather, she was in a certain way a star of the night; hence, a star shone even in the distant night when she gave birth. Seeing it the Magi from the Orient were able to adore the light. Thus the words "the light shone out of the darkness" was realized for them also.

St. Augustine of Hippo, IV century

PRAYER

I have nothing to offer you,
nothing to ask from you.
I come only, O Mother, to contemplate you.
Because you are beautiful,
because you are immaculate,
the woman of grace finally restored,
as she came from God
on the morning of her original splendor.
It is simply because you exist,
O Mother of Jesus Christ,
that you are thanked!

Paul Claudel (1868-1955)

MARY, QUEEN OF MARTYRS

From the Gospel according to Matthew (2:16-18)

When Herod saw that he had been tricked by the wise men, he was infuriated, and he sent and had killed all the children in and around Bethlehem who were two years old or under, according to the time that he had learned from the wise men. Thus was fulfilled what had been spoken through the prophet Jeremiah:
"A voice was heard in Ramah,
wailing and loud lamentations,
Rachel weeping for her children;
she refused to be consoled, because they are no more."

Comment

God is powerless and weak in the world. In this way, and only in this way, does he remain with us and helps us. Christ helps us not so much by virtue of his omnipotence, but by virtue of his suffering.

Dietrich Bonhoeffer (1906-1945)

PRAYER

O holy Virgin,
you have generated in the flesh the Word.
Sanctify our souls, grant us to live in fidelity,
we who always praise you and acclaim:
"Save us, O gate of salvation,
protect us, O mother of truth,
help us who honor you, O immaculate one!
Keep the numerous potential downfalls far from us,
O most pure one!
Protect, defend, and keep those who hope in you!"

Sergius I, Patriarch of Constantinople,
VII century

MARY,
OBEDIENT WOMAN

From the Gospel according to Luke (2:48-50)

When his parents saw him they were astonished; and his mother said to him, "Son, why have you treated us this way? Look, your father and I have been searching for you in great anxiety." He said to them, "Why were you searching for me? Did you not know that I must be in my Father's house?" But they did not understand what he said to them.

Comment

How great and how heroic is the obedience of faith shown by Mary in the face of the inscrutable judgments of God! How she abandons herself to God without reserve, lending the full homage of her intellect and will to Him whose ways are inaccessible! And at the same time how powerful is the action of grace in her soul, how penetrating the influence of the Holy Spirit, his light and his virtue! By means of this faith Mary is perfectly united with Christ.

St. Pope John Paul II

PRAYER

Mary, mother of Jesus,
give me your heart,
so beautiful, so pure, so immaculate,
so full of love and humility:
make me capable of receiving Jesus in the bread of life,
of loving him as you have loved him and have served him,
in the poor garments of the poorest of the poor.
Amen.

Bl. Mother Teresa of Calcutta (1910-1997)

MARY
OF NAZARETH

From the Gospel according to Mark (6:1-3)

He left that place and came to his home town, and his disciples followed him. On the Sabbath he began to teach in the synagogue, and many who heard him were astounded. They said, "Where did this man get all this? What is this wisdom that has been given to him? What deeds of power are being done by his hands! Is not this the carpenter, the son of Mary and brother of James and Joses and Judas and Simon, and are not his sisters here with us!?" And they took offence at him.

Comment

Tell me: Who is that carpenter who has made the world from nothing? Who is that carpenter who invented art itself? Therefore, O reader, you can call him a "carpenter," provided you confess that he is the "Son of God;" you can call him the "Son of Mary" saying also that he is a "true man," provided you confess that he is the "Son of a virgin." You may also talk of "brothers;" in this way affirming and declaring the immense condescension of the Creator.

Peter Chrysologus, V century

PRAYER

O holy Mary, worker woman,
perhaps you alone can understand
that this our foolishness of bringing you back
to the confines of the down-to-earth experiences
of our lives is not a sign of irreverent manners...
Come walk discretely with us,
O extraordinary creature in love with normality,
who before being crowned queen of heaven,
swallowed the dust of our poor earth.

Tonino Bello (1935-1993)

MARY,
WOMAN OF THE NEW WINE

From the Gospel according to John (2:1-5)

There was a wedding in Cana of Galilee, and the mother of Jesus was there. Jesus and his disciples had also been invited to the wedding. When the wine ran out, the mother of Jesus said to him, "They have no wine." And Jesus said to her, "Woman, what concern is that to you and to me? My hour has not yet come." His mother said to the servants, "Do whatever he tells you."

Comment

When Christ by his power publicly changed the water into wine, the whole crowd was filled with joy, finding the taste of that wine to be very pleasant. Today we can all sit at the banquet of the Church, because the wine is changed into the blood of Christ and we all partake of it in holy joy, glorifying the great Spouse. Because the true Spouse is the Son of Mary, the Word that exists from all eternity, who has assumed the condition of a slave and has created everything with wisdom.

Romanos the Melodist, VI century

PRAYER

O you, who in your power
have changed water into wine,
change into joy
the oppressive sadness of my sins,
through the Theotokos;
O Christ, God,
you who have created everything with wisdom.

Romanos the Melodist, VI century

MARY, BLESSED BECAUSE SHE HAS BELIEVED

From the Gospel according to Luke (11:27-28)

While he was saying this, a woman in the crowd raised her voice and said to him, "Blessed is the womb that bore you and the breasts that nursed you!" But he said, "Blessed rather are those who hear the word of God and obey it."

Comment

Mary is blessed because she has listened to the word of God and has put it into practice. In fact, she has kept the truth more in her mind than in her flesh. Christ is truth, Christ is flesh; Christ is truth in the mind of Mary, Christ is flesh in the womb of Mary. What she carries in her mind counts for more than what she carries in her womb.

St. Augustine of Hippo, IV century

PRAYER

O blessed Mary,
let our prayers enter
the sanctuary of your hearing.
Accept what we offer you,
give us what we ask for,
forgive what we fear.
Holy Mary, be near and respond promptly
to the voice of one imploring you.
Let it be your work
to pray unceasingly
for favor for the people of God,
O Blessed One,
who have merited
to generate the ransom
of the world.

From a homily of
Alan of Farfa,
VIII century

MARY,
WOMAN OF THE CROSS

From the Gospel according to John (19:25-27)

Standing near the cross of Jesus was his mother, his mother's sister, Mary the wife of Clopas, and Mary Magdalene. When Jesus saw his mother and the disciple whom he loved standing beside her, he said to his mother, "Woman, here is your son." Then he said to the disciple, "Here is your mother." And from that hour the disciple took her into his own home.

Comment

The first thing to do, the most important of all, is not to be near the cross generally, but to stay near the cross "of Jesus." It is not enough to stay near the cross, that is, simply to suffer; even to stay there in silence. No. While this alone already seems to be an heroic thing, yet it is not the most important thing. Indeed, it can be nothing. The decisive thing is to stay near the cross "of Jesus." What counts is not the suffering, but the believing. The first thing is faith.

Raniero Cantalamessa

PRAYER

We are united in prayer with you,
Mother of Christ: with you,
who have shared in his sufferings.
You lead us to the Heart of your Son
agonizing on the cross
when, in his stripping,
he is revealed to the very end as Love.
O you who have shared in his sufferings,
allow us to persevere always
in the embrace of this mystery.

Mother of the Redeemer!
Lead us close to the Heart of your Son!

St. Pope John Paul II

MARY,
QUEEN OF THE APOSTLES

From the Acts of the Apostles (1:12-14)

Then they returned to Jerusalem from the mount called Olivet (...) When they had entered the city, they went to the room upstairs where they were staying, Peter, and John, and James, and Andrew, Philip and Thomas, Bartholomew and Matthew, James the son of Alphaeus, and Simon the Zealot, and Judas the son of James. All these were constantly devoting themselves to prayer, together with certain women, including Mary the mother of Jesus, as well as his brothers.

Comment

Mary has given Jesus Christ to the world. She showed him to Joseph, to the shepherds, to John the Baptist, to the gentile peoples. She presented Jesus at the temple, she showed him at Nazareth, revealed him as wisdom of the Father to the doctors, showed him to the apostles at the wedding in Cana, showed him crucified on Calvary: salvation for the whole world on Calvary. She showed him again returning to the Father on Ascension Day; she presented him to all the followers... She will show us Jesus when we enter Paradise. Because of this Mary is the apostle, the Queen of Apostles, the exemplar in every apostolate, the inspirer of all the apostolic virtues.

James Alberione (1884-1971)

PRAYER

Hail, perennial voice of the apostles;
Hail, indomitable daring of the martyrs.
Hail, powerful sustainer of the faith;
Hail, resplendent flag of grace.
Hail, because of you hell was despoiled;
Hail, because of you we were vested with glory.
Hail, Virgin and Spouse!

Text taken from the Akathistos
of the Oriental Church

MARY,
ASSUMED INTO HEAVEN

From a 7th century panegyric on the Dormition

A strong sound from heaven was heard towards nine in the morning and a perfume floated that was so sweet that all the bystanders were overcome by sleep except for the apostles and the three virgins, to whom the Lord had granted the privilege to stay awake... And behold the Lord came on the clouds with a countless multitude of angels... Taking her soul, they laid it on the hands of Michael, after having wrapped it in something resembling animal pelts, the splendor of which it is impossible to describe. The apostles contemplated the soul of Mary, seven times brighter than the sun, which was entrusted to the hands of Michael.

Comment

It is quite possible that the resurrection of the Mother of God may have preceded the resurrection of the others, as a forerunner of their resurrection: during her earthly life she already had preceded them in merits. We should not doubt that she died as her son, who assumed our humanity, also died. But she did not remain in death for long. He who had taken flesh from her had defeated death through his resurrection; her son, who ascended into heaven with majesty, certainly had the power to draw his mother to himself. There is no doubt that he gave her a share in his glory and made her Queen of the whole world.

Atto of Vercelli, X century

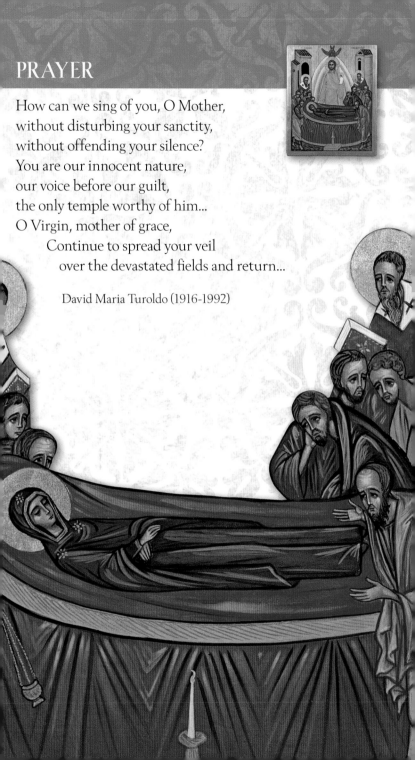

PRAYER

How can we sing of you, O Mother,
without disturbing your sanctity,
without offending your silence?
You are our innocent nature,
our voice before our guilt,
the only temple worthy of him...
O Virgin, mother of grace,
    Continue to spread your veil
        over the devastated fields and return...

David Maria Turoldo (1916-1992)

MARY, QUEEN OF THE WORLD

From the Book of Revelation (12:1-2, 5)

A great portent appeared in heaven: a woman clothed with the sun, with the moon under her feet, and on her head a crown of twelve stars. She was pregnant and was crying out in birth pangs, in the agony of giving birth. (...) She gave birth to a son, a male child, who is to rule all the nations with a rod of iron.

Comment

The woman symbolizes holy Church... She is justly described as clothed with the sun, because she received in promise the Christ, the true sun of justice. The moon is under her feet, because the brilliance of temporal goods falls under her rule. The son of the woman, that is, the son of the Church, of the virgin woman Mary, was carried away up to God and to his throne and from there, looking down, he derides all the heads of the dragon, as the Holy Spirit has said in the psalm, "He who inhabits the heavens will laugh at them and the Lord will mock them. Then he will speak to them in his anger, and in his fury he will confound them, saying: 'I myself have established my king in Sion' (Ps 2:4-6)."

Rupert of Deutz, XII century

PRAYER

I greet you, O blessed Virgin,
who have defeated evil,
spouse of the Most High and mother
of the gentle Lamb;
you reign in heaven and save the earth.
Men lean towards you
while the demons fear you.
You are the star that shines in the east
and dissipates the darkness in the west,
the dawn that announces the sun,
and the day that knows not the night.

Peter the Venerable, abbot of Cluny,
XII century

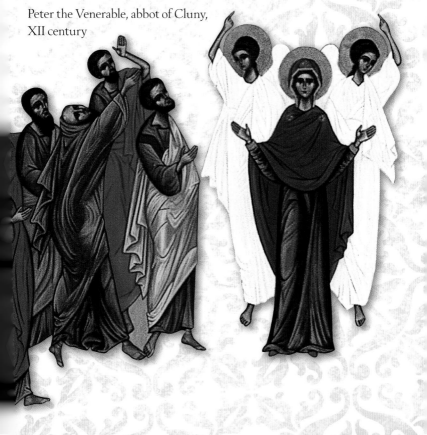

Mother of Mercy: A Month with Mary

Original title: Madre di misericordia: Un mese con Maria,
© 2010, Edizioni San Paolo s.r.l.
– Cinisello Balsamo, Milan, Italy

Icons of: Sr. Marie-Paul Farran. Bénédictines de Notre Dame du Calvaire.
Jerusalem, Mount of Olives

Translated into English by Arthur Palisada SSP and Michael Goonan SSP

The Scripture quotations contained herein are adapted from the New Revised
Standard Version Bible, copyright © 1989. Division of Christian Education
of the National Council of Churches of Christ in the U.S.A. Used with
permission. All rights reserved.

English language edition © 2015 St. Pauls Publications,
PO Box 906, Strathfield NSW 2135, Australia

North American edition published by
ST PAULS
2187 Victory Boulevard
Staten Island, New York 10314
www.stpauls.us

ISBN 978-0-8189-1390-7

St Pauls Publications is an activity of the priests and brothers of the Society
of St. Paul who place at the center of their lives the mission of evangelization
through the means of social communication.